Anteaters, Bats & Boas

The **AMAZON RAINFOREST** from the **FOREST FLOOR** to the **TREETOPS**

ROXIE MUNRO

HOLIDAY HOUSE · NEW YORK

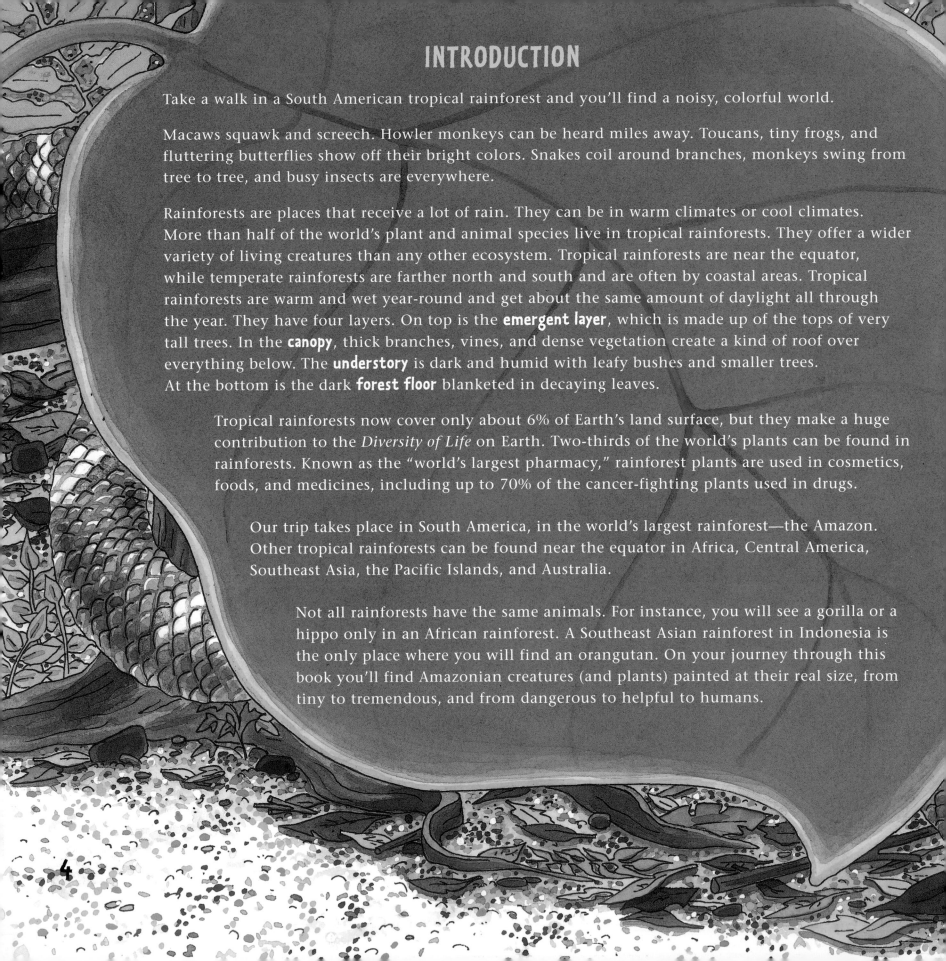

INTRODUCTION

Take a walk in a South American tropical rainforest and you'll find a noisy, colorful world.

Macaws squawk and screech. Howler monkeys can be heard miles away. Toucans, tiny frogs, and fluttering butterflies show off their bright colors. Snakes coil around branches, monkeys swing from tree to tree, and busy insects are everywhere.

Rainforests are places that receive a lot of rain. They can be in warm climates or cool climates. More than half of the world's plant and animal species live in tropical rainforests. They offer a wider variety of living creatures than any other ecosystem. Tropical rainforests are near the equator, while temperate rainforests are farther north and south and are often by coastal areas. Tropical rainforests are warm and wet year-round and get about the same amount of daylight all through the year. They have four layers. On top is the **emergent layer**, which is made up of the tops of very tall trees. In the **canopy**, thick branches, vines, and dense vegetation create a kind of roof over everything below. The **understory** is dark and humid with leafy bushes and smaller trees. At the bottom is the dark **forest floor** blanketed in decaying leaves.

Tropical rainforests now cover only about 6% of Earth's land surface, but they make a huge contribution to the *Diversity of Life* on Earth. Two-thirds of the world's plants can be found in rainforests. Known as the "world's largest pharmacy," rainforest plants are used in cosmetics, foods, and medicines, including up to 70% of the cancer-fighting plants used in drugs.

Our trip takes place in South America, in the world's largest rainforest—the Amazon. Other tropical rainforests can be found near the equator in Africa, Central America, Southeast Asia, the Pacific Islands, and Australia.

Not all rainforests have the same animals. For instance, you will see a gorilla or a hippo only in an African rainforest. A Southeast Asian rainforest in Indonesia is the only place where you will find an orangutan. On your journey through this book you'll find Amazonian creatures (and plants) painted at their real size, from tiny to tremendous, and from dangerous to helpful to humans.

Emerald tree boas are born red or orange, but after a year, they turn green. These snakes are beautiful, but rarely move from their perches. They stay coiled or looped over a tree branch, spending days or even weeks digesting their dinners, which can be mice, lizards, bats, or even monkeys.

Not all creatures with legs walk. **Brown-throated three-toed sloths** move very slowly. They inch along upside down on the undersides of branches. They do a lot of resting to digest their food. It can take them up to a month to fully digest a big meal. They can swim well, but because of their hooked claws, weak back legs, and extra-long front legs, they can barely walk on the ground.

The **black-eared fairy hummingbird** is the opposite of slow. Its wings can beat up to 80 times a second. It can fly forward and backward, and can even hover like a helicopter. Its feet are tiny, and although it can use them to perch on twigs, like most hummingbirds, it cannot walk.

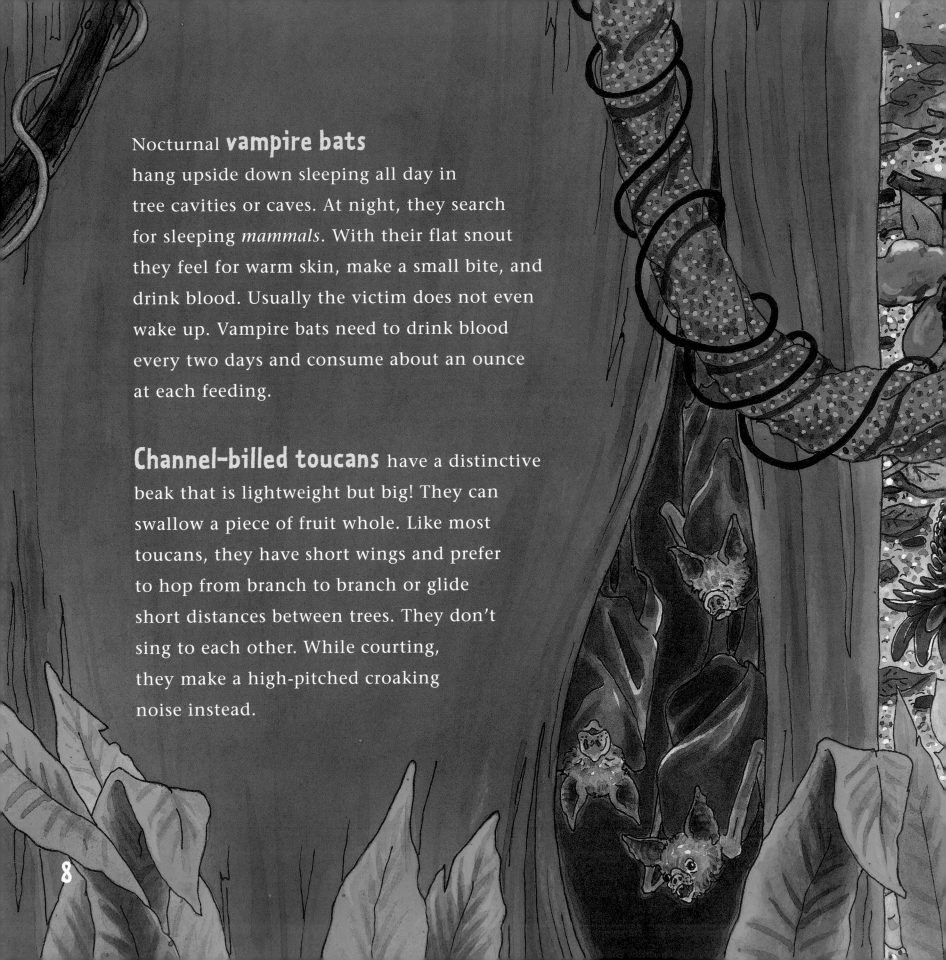

Nocturnal **vampire bats** hang upside down sleeping all day in tree cavities or caves. At night, they search for sleeping *mammals*. With their flat snout they feel for warm skin, make a small bite, and drink blood. Usually the victim does not even wake up. Vampire bats need to drink blood every two days and consume about an ounce at each feeding.

Channel–billed toucans have a distinctive beak that is lightweight but big! They can swallow a piece of fruit whole. Like most toucans, they have short wings and prefer to hop from branch to branch or glide short distances between trees. They don't sing to each other. While courting, they make a high-pitched croaking noise instead.

There's gold in the rainforest! **Golden lion tamarins** are little monkeys that live in family groups of two to eight individuals. They will eat just about anything smaller than they are: fruits, insects, and small animals. Their long, skinny fingers help them reach into hiding places to catch their snacks.

The **eyelash viper** has dramatic eyes. It hunts mostly at night, sitting and waiting in low-hanging branches and vines for frogs, lizards, baby birds, bats, or *rodents* to come close. Then it strikes with lightning speed and injects a powerful *venom*. Because they are bright yellow, they are sometimes accidentally shipped all over the world with bananas!

This vivid **yellow-banded**, or **bumblebee, poison dart frog,** has adhesive pads on its toes and fingertips, which help it attach to plant surfaces. Its bright colors warn other animals that it secretes poison through its skin.

The **green iguana** is a giant *reptile* that can climb up high in the canopy. It looks fierce but is really a shy vegetarian that runs away when scared, sometimes by jumping from a tree into the water or onto the ground. It moves fast—up to 35 miles an hour, or 56 kilometers per hour, speedier than most galloping racehorses.

Leaf-cutter ants can carry up to 50 times their weight. That's like a human carrying a hippopotamus! Like iguanas, they are vegetarians. But they don't eat the leaves they bring home. They use them to grow fungus (including mini-mushrooms) for dinner. They're farmers!

13

Many insects with unique legs inhabit the floor and understory of the rainforest. **Blue morpho butterflies**, like all butterflies, have taste sensors in their legs. They stand on their food and taste it with their feet. They are some of the largest butterflies in the world, with wingspans of 5 to 7 inches (13 to 18 centimeters).

Brightly colored little **Amazon leaf-footed bugs** are *herbivores*, and particularly like fruits and plant sap. They might raise up their wild looking back legs to scare off predators.

Giant yellow-legged centipedes don't actually have 100 legs ("centi" means *one hundred* in Latin and "ped" means *foot*). Centipedes can have between 30 and more than 300 legs. These *invertebrates* have a nasty venomous bite, too, so stay away!

Small **Amazon bluewing dragonflies** can hover in the air like helicopters, or fly straight up and down. Dragonflies look delicate, but they are among the fastest insects on Earth. Some can fly up to 50 miles per hour, or 80 kilometers per hour.

The fuzzy **pink-toed tarantula** is nocturnal, hiding until night. It has stiff hairs all over its body, and fangs with a venom that is harmless to humans. The females are larger than the males and can have a leg span of up to nearly five inches (13 centimeters).

Furry multicolored **giant anteaters** have no teeth. Their tongues are two feet (2/3 meters) long and can flick up to 160 times a minute, lapping up to 35,000 ants or termites in one day! They have poor eyesight, but as their long noses suggest, they have a super sense of smell that's 40 times greater than a human's.

Like many rainforest creatures, the scary-looking **rhinoceros beetle** and the big-eyed **mouse opossum** are named after other animals. The rhinoceros beetle is harmless to humans—it can't bite or sting. The mouse opossum, like some spider monkeys, has a *prehensile* tail, which helps it climb trees. Mouse opossums are small—only 5 to 8 inches (12 to 18 centimeters) long, including their tails.

Giant armadillos can grow up to 5 feet (1 1/2 meters) long. They carry their own defensive armor—a leathery shell made up of overlapping plates. Their long, sharp front claws help them dig out termites and ants from mounds. They have up to a hundred teeth—more than any other mammal.

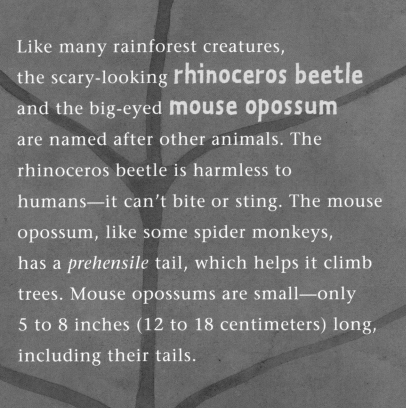

Schneider's smooth-fronted caiman is about 7 feet, or 2 to 3 meters, long. They lay their eggs near or on top of termite mounds to keep them an even temperature. You can see large distinctive scutes (bony or horny plates) on this caiman's back.

There are more than 220 poison dart frog species in the Amazon. The tiny **Sira poison dart frog** isn't as dangerous as some of its frog cousins, which are among the most toxic animals on Earth. The more brilliant the color of a rainforest frog, the more powerful is its venom. One lick, and a *predator* could die. So this guy is pretty scary for its size!

Such colorful patterns! This good-looking **red-footed tortoise**, found throughout South America, can live to be 60 years old. It has chirpy mating calls that sound like a chicken clucking!

Rainforests are full of butterflies, like these **Julia butterflies**. Male Julia butterflies often drink the tears of caimans and turtles, called "tear-feeding," in order to get the salt they need. A swarm (or group) of butterflies like this is called a "kaleidoscope."

There are more kinds of beetles than any other animal on Earth— almost 500,000. Most beetle species live in rainforests, like this big beautiful **metallic wood-boring beetle**.

24

Macaws, like this **blue-winged macaw**, are large parrots. They are social animals whose loud squawks, screams, and screeches communicate with their flock.

Another beautiful blue creature flapping its wings is this swallowtail, known as a **blue doctor**. Unlike the noisy and social macaw, this delicate butterfly is quiet and is often found alone.

A **jaguar's** fur pattern *camouflages* it in the dappled forest light. It is a superb climber, and often lies on a big tree branch to rest or sleep. Unlike most cats, jaguars love the water and are excellent swimmers.

26

Brown-capped capuchins are smart. They have complex vocal sounds for communicating. These primates are the most dexterous of all the monkeys. They use tools, like stones, to crack open nuts. Agile jumpers, they can leap 9 feet, or almost 3 meters, from branch to branch. They are dangerous predators and hunt other monkeys, as well as birds, bats, insects, lizards, and frogs.

A **praying mantis** is tougher than it looks. It is strong, with "spikes" on its arms to capture and hold prey. It has excellent eyesight, and can rotate its head almost 360 degrees. A camouflage expert, it blends in with the leaf it's perched on. Mantises jump too—not as far as monkeys, but much faster, in the blink of an eye. In the Amazon, mantises can be up to a foot long, or 30 centimeters, and can catch a hummingbird and eat it!

The **harpy eagle** has a
wingspan of 7 feet, or about 2 meters,
and is one of the world's largest eagles.
They are *carnivores* that hunt monkeys
and sloths in the canopy and occasionally
on the ground. Then they fly back to
their nests in the emergent trees high above
the rainforest canopy to feed their young.

1. EMERALD TREE BOA

2. BROWN-THROATED THREE-TOED SLOTHS

3. BLACK-EARED FAIRY HUMMINGBIRD

4. VAMPIRE BATS

5. CHANNEL-BILLED TOUCAN

6. GOLDEN LION TAMARINS

7. EYELASH VIPER

8. YELLOW-BANDED, OR BUMBLEBEE, POISON DART FROG

9. GREEN IGUANA

10. LEAF-CUTTER ANTS

11. BLUE MORPHO BUTTERFLY

12. AMAZON LEAF-FOOTED BUGS

13. GIANT YELLOW-LEGGED CENTIPEDES

14. AMAZON BLUEWING DRAGONFLIES

15. PINK-TOED TARANTULA

16. GIANT ANTEATER

17. RHINOCEROS BEETLE

18. MOUSE OPOSSUM

MAMMALS (PINK)

BIRDS (BLUE)

REPTILES (GREEN)

AMPHIBIANS (PURPLE)

INSECTS (YELLOW)

ARACHNIDS (ORANGE)

CENTIPEDES (TURQUOISE)

The Layers of the Rainforest

Emergent layer: This highest layer is made up of the tops of giant trees that grow up above the canopy where their leaves can capture a lot of sunlight. It is home to birds, bats, and butterflies.

Canopy: In this layer thick branches, vines, and leaves intertwine to form a kind of roof that shades everything below. Small plants, including orchids and ferns, grow on the trees. It's home to more birds, reptiles, mammals, and insects than any other layer.

Understory: Smaller trees and bushes grow in this hot, humid layer. Some plants here have large leaves to collect sunlight in this dark zone. Jaguars, birds, *amphibians*, and insects live here.

Forest floor: Dead leaves and branches litter the ground of this bottom layer. *Decomposers*, including insects, worms, and fungi, help break down the litter into nutrients. Reptiles, amphibians, birds, and large and small mammals, including humans, also live here.

Preserving Rainforests

Think of a football field. Pretty big, right? Every *hour* in the Amazon rainforest, areas up to the size of 4,000 football fields are cleared of timber or burned. The land is being used for mining, lumber production, ranching, or farms. Humans have already demolished 20% of the Amazon rainforest, and if this continues, in fifty years the whole rainforest will be gone. Rainforests in other parts of the world, including Indonesia and the Congo Basin in Africa, are also being destroyed.

We need rainforests! Rainforests make up the world's oldest living ecosystem on land. They produce the oxygen we breathe, special plants for medicines, and many of the world's foods. They absorb the greenhouse gases that accelerate global warming and create more extreme weather patterns. Rainforests help keep water cycles healthy because their plants hold lots of moisture. The loss of those plants makes the climate drier and creates droughts.

Seventy percent of the world's plants and land animals live in rainforests, including 150 species of migratory birds that travel to the Amazon yearly from North America. But every day, many NEW species of animals are killed off before they are even discovered and named—made extinct before we even know about them!

People all over the world are working hard to preserve those rainforests that still remain. It is vitally important that they be protected, and that the fascinating animals and valuable plants of the rainforest be allowed to live.

GLOSSARY

Amphibian: A vertebrate animal that can live in and out of water and that needs to keep its skin moist all the time. Frogs, salamanders, and toads are amphibians.

Camouflage: The patterns, shapes, or colors an animal uses to conceal itself or blend in with the background.

Carnivore: An animal that eats the flesh of other animals. A meat eater.

Decomposers: Organisms that break down dead or decaying organic material such as dead animals, wood, and waste. They are sometimes called "Earth's clean-up crew." Termites, earthworms, fungi, and bacteria are decomposers.

Diversity of Life: The huge variety of living organisms, from tiny to tremendous, on Earth. All plants and animals in their particular habitats and ecosystems.

Herbivore: An animal that eats plants, a vegetarian. Grazing animals such as cattle and giraffes are herbivores.

Invertebrate: Animals without backbones such as insects and centipedes.

Mammal: A warm-blooded vertebrate animal that usually has hair or fur and feeds its young with milk. Humans, dogs, and mice are mammals.

Predator: An animal that hunts, catches, and eats other animals.

Prehensile: A body part that can grasp an object, like a human's hand or a chimpanzee's foot.

Reptiles: Cold-blooded vertebrates, like snakes, turtles, and lizards.

Rodent: A mammal with front teeth that continually grow, so it constantly gnaws to keep them short. Mice, squirrels, and hamsters are rodents.

Venom: Chemicals, like poison, that animals that sting or bite can use to paralyze prey or predators.

Vertebrates: Animals with a backbone. Reptiles, birds, amphibians, fishes, and mammals are vertebrates.

LEARN MORE ABOUT RAINFORESTS

Reference Books

Dragonflies. Pieter Van Dokkum. Yale University Press/New Haven & London, 2015.

Frogs. David Badger. Voyager Press, Stillwater, MN, 1995.

The Primate Family Tree. Ian Redmond. Foreword, Jane Goodall. Firefly Books, 2011.

Wildlife of the World. Dr. Don E. Wilson. Smithsonian, DK/Penguin Random House, NY, NY, 2015.

Children's Books

24 Hours: Rain Forest. Fleur Stur. DK Publishing, NY, NY, 2006.

The Great Kapok Tree: A Tale of the Amazon Rain Forest. Lynne Cherry. Voyager Books, Harcourt, NY, NY, 1990.

Rain Forest. Elinor Greenwood. DK Publishing, NY, NY, 2001.

The Rainforest Grew All Around. Susan K. Mitchell, illustrated by Connie McLennan. Sylvan Dell Publishing, Mt Pleasant, SC, 2007.

A Rainforest Habitat. Molly Aloian and Bobbie Kalman. Crabtree Publishing, NY, NY, 2012.

Rain Forests. Marge Ferguson Delano. National Geographic Kids, Washington, DC, 2017.

Reptiles. Dr. Allen E. Greer. Time-Life Books. 1996.

Tropical Rainforests. Seymour Simon. Smithsonian, Harper Collins, NY, NY, 2010.

Websites

Rainforest Action Network: https://www.ran.org/

Rainforest Alliance: https://www.rainforest-alliance.org/

Smithsonian Institution: https://forestgeo.si.edu/ecological-zone/tropical-rainforest

Virtual Rainforest (NSF and MSU): http://www.virtual-rainforest.org/

INDEX

To all the people working to preserve the world's rainforests

The publisher would like to thank Dr. Laura K. Marsh,
Director and Co-Founder of the Global Conservation Institute.

Copyright © 2021 by Roxie Munro
All Rights Reserved
HOLIDAY HOUSE is registered in the U.S. Patent and Trademark Office.
Printed and bound in April 2021 at C&C Offset, Shenzhen, China.
The artwork was created with India ink and colored acrylic inks on
100% cotton rag paper.
www.holidayhouse.com
First Edition
1 3 5 7 9 10 8 6 4 2

Library of Congress Cataloging-in-Publication Data

Names: Munro, Roxie, author. | Title: Anteaters, bats, and boas : the Amazon
rainforest from the treetops to the forest floor / Roxie Munro.
Description: First edition. | New York : Holiday House, [2021]
Includes bibliographical references and index. | Audience: Ages 4–8
Audience: Grades K–1 | Summary: "Bright, realistic illustrations of a busy Amazon
rain forest depict a plethora of creatures, all drawn to size, going about their daily
lives"—Provided by publisher. | Identifiers: LCCN 2020039144
ISBN 9780823446568 (hardcover) | Subjects: LCSH: Rain forest animals—Amazon
River Region—Juvenile literature.
Classification: LCC QL235 .M86 2021 | DDC 591.7340981/1—dc23
LC record available at https://lccn.loc.gov/2020039144
ISBN: 978-0-8234-4656-8 (hardcover)

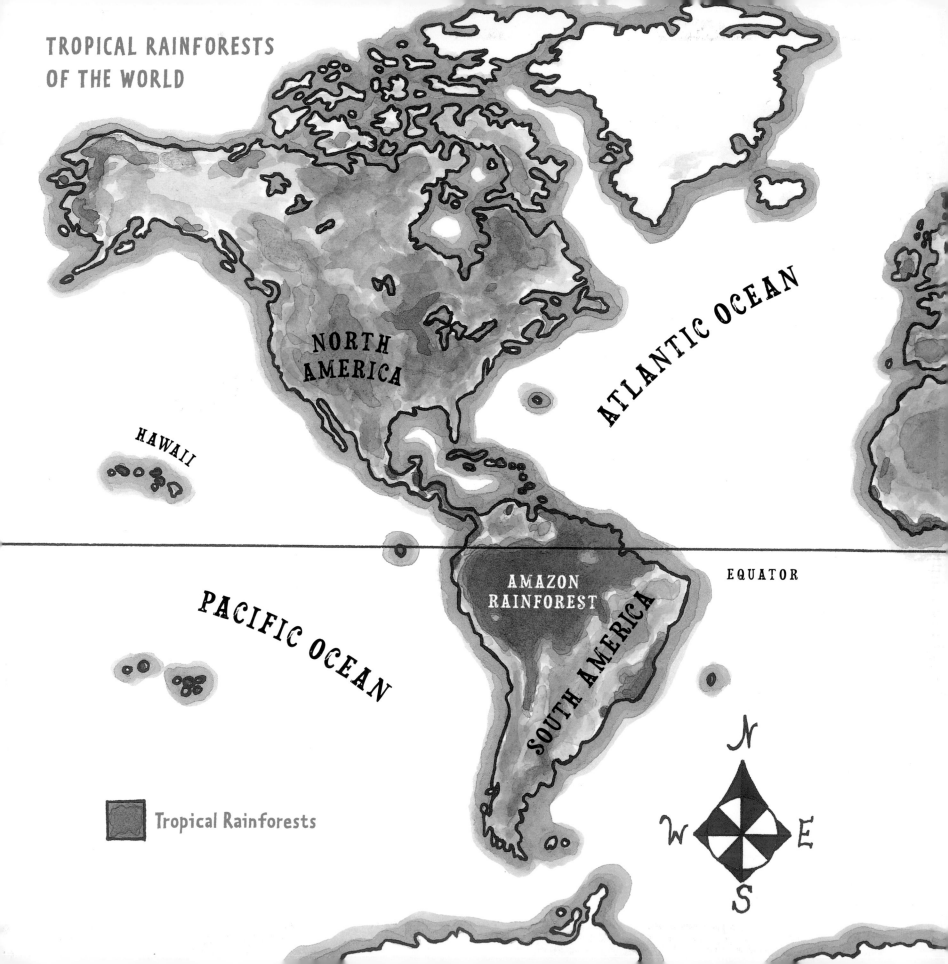